TRAIN OUR HANDS TO

TRAIN OUR HANDS TO

A PRACTICAL GUIDE TO OVERCOMING
THE MANY CHALLENGES OF LIFE

MIN. DEBBIE REID

All scriptures quoted are from the King James Version of the Bible unless otherwise noted.

Train Our Hands to War

ISBN: 979-8-9868965-0-2

Copyright © 2022 Min. Debbie Reid

All publishing rights belong exclusively to Penned for Purpose Publishing

Cover Design – Kenya Gould, Designs By Kenya, kenya@designsbykenya.com

All rights reserved.

No portion of this book may be reproduced or stored in a retrieval system, or transmitted in any form or by any means, except for brief quotations in printed reviews, without the prior permission of the author.

Printed in the United States of America

TRAIN OUR HANDS TO

A PRACTICAL GUIDE TO OVERCOMING
THE MANY CHALLENGES OF LIFE

MIN. DEBBIE REID

All scriptures quoted are from the King James Version of the Bible unless otherwise noted.

Train Our Hands to War

ISBN: 979-8-9868965-0-2

Copyright © 2022 Min. Debbie Reid

All publishing rights belong exclusively to Penned for Purpose Publishing

Cover Design – Kenya Gould, Designs By Kenya, kenya@designsbykenya.com

All rights reserved.

No portion of this book may be reproduced or stored in a retrieval system, or transmitted in any form or by any means, except for brief quotations in printed reviews, without the prior permission of the author.

Printed in the United States of America

DEDICATION

This is dedicated to my loving children,
Tiana Marable and Wanya Smith
My supportive husband, Michael Reid
My amazing parents, Letcher and Virginia Marable
And my brothers, Alfonza and Jerome Marable

When you are going through struggles in life, there is nothing like a tribe encamped around you. Family above everything...each of you are my tribe.
I love you dearly!

ACKNOWLEDGEMENTS

I would like to take a moment to extend my love and appreciation to those in my tribe who never stopped supporting me in all of my creative endeavors.

Thank You, God, for being everything to me and for giving me the giftings and talents to be used for Your kingdom work. Thank You for still having a purpose for me. I pray You continue to empty me because when You call me home, I want You to say "She emptied herself of every gifting, every talent, every ounce of human love she had to give while here on earth."

To my entire family, thank you for the unyielding love you provide to me. Family is extremely important, and you know my motto is "family over everything."

Thank you to the family I have acquired outside of blood. There are far too many of you to name. If you are reading this acknowledgement, and we are kindred

ACKNOWLEDGEMENTS

spirits—thank you! God has placed us in the trenches so that together we can come out victorious!

Special Thank You:

To my writing coach, Prophetess Tiffany McKoy, for encouraging me in your first Wind Writing Class. I was so proud to be a part of the very first cohort. This book is being birthed earlier than expected because of your encouragement, discipline, and direction!

To my graphic artist, Kenya Gould, who took my vision and brought it to life in such a way that even I didn't expect. The cover is amazing! And, to my dear editor, Francheska White. From my first meeting with you, I was blessed. I knew God had a divine appointment over our connection and I continue to feel it with each encounter.

To my inner circle, Shatisha Parker, Kayleigh McLean, Cashmeira Henderson, Dr. Gladys Forte, Evangelist LaToya Bryant and Prophetess Doneta Dawson, thank you for encouraging me through the writing process and for taking time out of your schedules to provide feedback

ACKNOWLEDGEMENTS

prior to publication. You ladies and the rest of our women's morning prayer group, aka 'The Council' have been such a joyous blessing! The prayers, the love and the support are unmatched!

To my Charlotte church family and Pastors John and Roslyn Das of Revive Church, and my Chicago church family and Pastor Dan and Lady Linda Willis of the Lighthouse Church of All Nations—thank you for always having my back in not only the spiritual things but life in general. I love each one of you immensely!

TABLE OF CONTENTS

DEDICATION	V
ACKNOWLEDGEMENTS	VII
INTRODUCTION	3
CHAPTER 1: OUR CHARACTER	11
1. AT THE READY	12
2. NOT EASILY ANGERED BUT QUICK IN PRAYER	17
3. GROUNDED IN HUMILITY	20
4. PASSIONATE	25
CHAPTER 2: OUR TOOLKITS	33
WEAPON 1: THE WORD OF GOD	35
WEAPON 2: PRAISE	37
WEAPON 3: PRAYER	41
GENERAL WARFARE	47

Deliverance	49
Provision	51
Healing	52
Peace	53
Repentance and Salvation	54
Praise	55
Faith	56
Blessings	58
Weapon 4: Fruit of the Spirit	60
Weapon 5: Faith	62

Chapter 3: Strategy — 67

Chapter 4: Battle Ready — 73

1. War Paint	78
2. War Stance	80
Posture of Your Heart	81
Posture of Surrender	83
Posture of Boldness	83
Posture of Obedience	85
3. War Cry	87

ACKNOWLEDGEMENTS

CHAPTER 5: REFUELING	*93*
MY PRAYER FOR YOU	*99*
APPENDIX	*105*
POWERFUL SCRIPTURES FOR SPIRITUAL WARFARE	*105*
WORDS OF WAR	*115*
NAMES OF GOD	*119*
NOTES	*125*
FAVORITE SCRIPTURES	*133*
PRAYERS	*141*
ABOUT THE AUTHOR	*149*

INTRODUCTION

*"Blessed be the L*ORD *my strength which teacheth my hands to war, and my fingers to fight: My goodness, and my fortress; my high tower, and my deliverer; my shield, and he in whom I trust; who subdueth my people under me."*

Psalm 144:1-2

INTRODUCTION

It's amazing how back in the day we didn't take anything from anyone. Like we were ready to posse up at the drop of a dime. I even remember when I was in high school, an individual had an issue with me...sweet little ol' me...LOL. Anyway, one day this young teen girl ran up to me in the high school hallway between classes wanting to fight. At that time, I was timid and shy...I was not the outgoing woman before you now. So, one of my closest, dearest friends jumped in the middle of the chaos. She looked at me and demanded that I go to class as the bell for the next period began to ring. I was taken aback, but as the studious person I was, I stepped away and went to class. It wasn't until the end of the day that I found out what had transpired after I stepped away. My ride or die took it upon herself to step in on my behalf and find this young lady that had an issue with me. I couldn't believe what I was hearing. Not only did she fight for me, but she also went to the principal's office and took the punishment for me! My mind was utterly blown! But isn't that what God does for us on a regular basis? He sees danger coming our way and is such an amazing Father that He tells us to go on about our day because He can handle the threats in front of us. What a mighty God we serve!

How can we have that type of protection around us and not be willing to fight for Him as well? He looks out for us in the natural, but He is also warring for us in the spiritual battles we face. When my friend stood up for me, she told me that it wasn't in my nature to fight or curse, so whenever I needed her, she would step in and do those things for me. Now I am not condoning physical altercations, but when someone rides that hard on your behalf, you cannot help but ride that hard for them in return. It's the same with God; we are always being protected from dangerous situations. Think about it. Have you ever been out driving and, for some reason, you randomly chose to take an alternate route? Have you ever planned to go somewhere and, at the last minute, changed your mind? Or have you ever wanted to make plans, but external forces completely disrupted them? Some of that may have been you and your choices, but I would also bet

INTRODUCTION

some of it was God intervening on your behalf because He saw the danger and redirected your steps. So, if we can devote undying love to a friend who goes to bat for us, why can't we show that same love and gratitude to God?

As I grew older, I didn't need my friend to fight my battles for me. I toughened up. I put on my big girl panties and went into survival mode. I mean, life happens. I got to the point where I didn't take anything from anyone. And if you came at me wrong, I was ready with my Vaseline and my hoodie (old school joke). I learned to not wear my heart on my sleeve and to stand up for what I believed. In the natural, I didn't take anything from anyone. I could hold my own when it came to physical fights, and I was a beast with my words. I could leave you thinking you were physically bleeding, yet I hadn't laid one hand on you. I am not glorifying being tough or fighting in the natural sense. I am laying the foundation for you to understand that my circumstances and choices ultimately developed my character. Just living life created this no-nonsense, thick-skinned, "don't play with me" persona where there was once such a meek, timid young lady.

INTRODUCTION

I know many of you can relate to going hard for the people that go hard for you. You are right there in the trenches with them, good, bad or indifferent. And don't let someone say something out of line or attack anyone you hold dear; a rush of adrenaline suddenly seeps in out of nowhere, overtakes you, and the beast is unleashed!

That was how I was with the people I loved, and truth be told how I still am. But then I realized if I could have that much passion for someone in the natural, why would I not give that attitude and more to God and to the things of God? I mean, you want to talk about the ultimate ride or die! When I changed the way I thought about things, something inside of me woke up. I realized that even if you give your all to a human being, they are still fallible and could end up letting you down.

Remember, Psalm 118:8 says, "It is better to trust in the LORD than to put confidence in man."

I am not writing this as an expert in spiritual warfare, nor am I professing to be the most studious Bible scholar. However, I am a survival expert. I hold a Ph.D. in life! I

INTRODUCTION

bring to you experiences, knowledge, wisdom, and understanding. If you want to understand how to fight the enemy, glean from someone who has done it time and time again and come out victorious!

CHAPTER 1

OUR CHARACTER

"Put on then, as God's chosen ones, holy and beloved, compassionate hearts, kindness, humility, meekness, and patience, bearing with one another and, if one has a complaint against another, forgiving each other; as the Lord has forgiven you, so you also must forgive. And above all these put on love, which binds everything together in perfect harmony. And let the peace of Christ rule in your hearts, to which indeed you were called in one body. And be thankful."

Colossians 3:12-15 (ESV)

CHAPTER 1: OUR CHARACTER

There are many different thoughts on the definition of a spiritual warrior. Some say being a Christian alone does not make you a spiritual warrior. Others say everyone faces battles in the spirit, so everyone essentially is a spiritual warrior. I don't have the answer one way or another, but God did inspire me with some of the many characteristics that define a spiritual warrior. This should help you draw your own conclusions as to whether you believe you are a spiritual warrior. If I would have to guess, I would say if you have fought battles in the natural that had some spiritual impact, then count yourself as a spiritual warrior and use this book to properly prepare yourself for future battles. This is not by any means a complete list of spiritual warrior characteristics, but it is a list of the four traits where I would like to focus our attention. Journey with me as we discuss these characteristics below:

CHAPTER 1: OUR CHARACTER

1. *At the Ready*

This is one of the first things God dropped in my spirit pertaining to being "at the ready." "Your character dictates your character – falsifying who you are for the sake of the public will falsify (confuse) who you are on the inside." Ephesians 5:6 states, "Let no one deceive you with empty words, for because of these things, the wrath of God comes upon the sons of disobedience."

What this says to me is the person you are (not the person you pretend to be) dictates the person you will eventually become in all areas. So, if you try to be something you are not, you eventually lose the person God created you to be, and you are no longer walking in truth but walking in a falsified persona. A perfect example of this would be an actor who plays a particular role. This actor has to lose themselves in that role in order to truly be successful. Sometimes, they play a role for so long that the lines become blurred, and they can no longer separate themselves from the person they portray on the screen. Essentially, you must know who you are and whose you are in order to understand your potential and God's

CHAPTER 1: OUR CHARACTER

power. Understanding this will allow you to prepare yourself better.

Continued preparation makes you always "at the ready." Will Smith coined the phrase, "If you stay ready, you don't have to get ready." This is quite powerful in spiritual warfare. Satan has one primary goal. 1 Peter 5:8 tells us, "Be sober, be vigilant; because your adversary the devil, as a roaring lion, walketh about, seeking whom he may devour."

Because of this fact, we know that we must be prepared at all times. It is essential in your victory. Luke 21:36 (Amplified) advises us, "But keep alert at all times [be attentive and ready], praying that you may have the strength and ability [to be found worthy and] to escape all these things that are going to take place, and to stand in the presence of the Son of Man [at His coming]."

A great example of this in the Bible is the story of Noah and the Ark found in Genesis chapters 5–9. I love Noah's story at this point in his life. I say "at this" point because, just like us, Noah was not a perfect man, and he made

CHAPTER 1: OUR CHARACTER

mistakes along the way. But when God gave him instructions, he was obedient without question. Can you imagine that? Being obedient to God without question?

God called on Noah to build an Ark in preparation (at the ready) for impending destruction over the earth. At this time, all mankind had become wicked in God's eyes. But Noah had great favor from God. Because of this favor, God gave him specific instructions on how to build the ark and who/what to bring aboard. Sometimes, everything around you can't go with you! That's a different topic for a different day. The miraculous thing about Noah's obedience was that he had never encountered rain before. Now, this is an argued point by many biblical scholars. But one thing is agreed on, there had never been a flood. He had no idea what to expect, but his faith in God was strong enough to warrant obedience. In Hebrews 11:7 (ESV), we are told that "By faith Noah, being warned by God concerning events as yet unseen, in reverent fear constructed an ark for the saving of his household. By this, he condemned the world and became an heir of the righteousness that comes by faith."

CHAPTER 1: OUR CHARACTER

"As yet seen" lets us know this was an event that had never been experienced before. How many of us would say we would obey God's instructions without hesitation if He told us something was going to happen that had never happened before on Earth? I dare say not many truthful hands would be raised. As the story goes, Noah followed God's instructions precisely. As a result, when God caused the great flood to wash over the earth and destroy everything in and on it, Noah, his family, and all animals on the Ark were spared.

This brings me to another amazing point of being "at the ready." God's exchange with Noah established a covenant that continues to exist between Him and us today. This covenant is known as the Noahic covenant. Our God honors our preparation if it is according to His plan and purpose for us. Noah's readiness still benefits us today. God's covenant to Noah was to never again destroy the earth and its inhabitants by a flood. He further reminds us of this promise every time we see a rainbow in the sky after it rains.

CHAPTER 1: OUR CHARACTER

We find this promise in Genesis 9:8-17 (ESV), "Then God said to Noah and to his sons with him, "Behold, I establish my covenant with you and your offspring after you, and with every living creature that is with you, the birds, the livestock, and every beast of the earth with you, as many as came out of the ark; it is for every beast of the earth. I establish my covenant with you, that never again shall all flesh be cut off by the waters of the flood, and never again shall there be a flood to destroy the earth." And God said, "This is the sign of the covenant that I make between you and me and every living creature that is with you, for all future generations: I have set my bow in the cloud, and it shall be a sign of the covenant between me and the earth. When I bring clouds over the earth, and the bow is seen in the clouds, I will remember my covenant that is between me and you and every living creature of all flesh. And the waters shall never again become a flood to destroy all flesh. When the bow is in the clouds, I will see it and remember the everlasting covenant between God and every living creature of all flesh that is on the earth." God said to Noah, 'This is the sign of the covenant that I have established between me and all flesh that is on the earth.'"

CHAPTER 1: OUR CHARACTER

2. Not easily angered but quick in prayer

Another important characteristic of a spiritual warrior is that he/she is not easily angered but is quick to pray. Many things in life are set up to anger us. God doesn't negate this. In His Word, God even tells us to be "slow to anger" and to "be angry but sin not." This is a powerful revelation. It is okay to get upset about things happening to you or going on around you but how you respond to that anger is crucial! A spiritual warrior will take their frustrations, hurt, and anger to God. Rather than blame God, they seek resolution from God through prayer.

Ephesians 6:18 (Amplified Version) says, "With all prayer and petition pray [with specific requests] at all times [on every occasion and in every season] in the Spirit, and with this in view, stay alert with all perseverance and petition [interceding in prayer] for all God's people."

I love that part of the latter scripture that says we should "pray at all times," meaning at any season of your life about all manner of things concerning not only you but for all of God's people. I remember a song I absolutely love

CHAPTER 1: OUR CHARACTER

entitled "A Praying Spirit," sung by one of my favorite gospel artists, Karen Clark-Sheard. I want God to give me a praying spirit throughout the day. This means that I want to be in a constant relationship with the Father! How amazing would that be? A praying spirit...a spirit that connects with God at all times and through anything we encounter. If we are that committed and that submitted to God, I would venture to say we would be more equipped to handle any challenges that come our way.

Let's take a brief look at the story of Hannah as it is written in 1 Samuel 1:2-2:21. Hannah was the mother of the prophet Samuel who we all know accomplished great things. But before she was known as Samuel's mother, she was first known for having a barren womb. Hannah would go to the temple of Shiloh to make sacrifices to the Lord and to pray for a child. This was her heart's desire. She was often ridiculed by Peninnah, the other wife of her husband, Elkanah. Peninnah had children, so she taunted Hannah for not being able to conceive. Even with all of the teasing she was receiving, Hannah did not allow her anger to turn her away from God. As a matter of fact, her desire to conceive was so strong that she wept in anguish before

CHAPTER 1: OUR CHARACTER

God, and she would not eat. In her pain, she remained consistent in prayer. Year after year, through her pain, anger, and frustration, she continued to pray to God to conceive a male child. She knew that God was the only one who could give her what she desired most in the world. Hannah made a promise to God. She told Him that if He would bless her with her heart's desire to have a son, she would dedicate the child back to Him. In God's time, He did indeed answer her prayer, and she gave birth to her first child. Furthermore, Hanna's first child was not her only child. She had a total of six children, four sons, and two daughters. When God is in the midst, not only does He answer our prayers but sometimes He multiplies them! Hanna's story is the epitome of James 5:16, which says, "Confess your faults one to another, and pray one for another, that ye may be healed. The effectual fervent prayer of a righteous man availeth much."

As a spiritual warrior, you must be willing to stay on the wall even if God does not seem to be answering your prayers. God will meet our consistency, effectuality, and fervency with blessings and favor. Another part of being quick in prayer...if you are talking to God in your most intimate, most vulnerable moments, you are refocusing and redirecting your attention away from the thing that caused anger to rise up in you. In turn, God releases you from that anger! A prayer warrior knows how to submit to an authority greater than themselves. The authority that has supreme authority!

3. Grounded in Humility

Humility is one of the basic building blocks of Christianity. The Bible gives us an example, "Now the man Moses was very meek, more than all people who were on the face of the earth (Numbers 12:3)."

But do not associate meekness with weakness; Moses was humble, but he was not weak. Paul was humble, but he was not weak. Joseph was humble, but he certainly was not weak. Speaking of Joseph, let's explore his story in Genesis 37-41. As you can see, the story of Joseph couldn't be contained in just one chapter; it spans four chapters. Clearly, we cannot detail every account of his life and the many lessons we can learn from it. But I will give you a very high-level understanding.

CHAPTER 1: OUR CHARACTER

Joseph is one of my absolute favorite characters in the Bible. His life inspires so many! To me, Jesus excluded, Joseph was one of the greatest examples of a spiritual warrior! His story is one of sibling rivalry, favoritism, revenge, famine, feast, and, greatest of all, forgiveness! He had many brothers, yet his father, Jacob, favored him. As you can imagine, this did not go over well with his other siblings. In retaliation for his father's favoritism and a dream that he shared with his brothers that seemed to imply he would one day rule over them. The brothers threw him in what many call a pit with the plan of leaving him to die, but they came across a caravan of Ishmaelites, so they decided to make a profit out of the selling of their brother instead. They took a precious coat given to Joseph by his father and dipped it in blood. They then showed this coat to their father, who then believed he was dead. Meanwhile, the 17-year-old Joseph had been sold as a slave to Potiphar, the captain of Pharoah's guard. Joseph found favor in Potiphar's home until Potiphar's wife made sexual advances toward the young man. Joseph refused her advances, so she lied to her husband by accusing him of sexual assault. This landed him in prison.

CHAPTER 1: OUR CHARACTER

"But the Lord was with Joseph and showed him steadfast love and gave him favor in the sight of the keeper of the prison. And the keeper of the prison put Joseph in charge of all the prisoners who were in prison. Whatever was done there, he was the one who did it. The keeper of the prison paid no attention to anything that was in Joseph's charge because the Lord was with him. And whatever he did, the Lord made it succeed" (Genesis 39:21-23 [ESV]).

While in prison, Joseph encountered a cupbearer and baker who had once worked for Pharaoh but were also imprisoned. They shared dreams with Joseph and discovered that he had a gift for interpreting dreams. This finding made its way back to King Pharaoh, who also had a troubling dream that needed to be interpreted. There is so much more to the story. Eventually, Joseph, who is age 30 at this point, gets out of prison and is blessed with one of the highest positions in the kingdom. King Pharoah's dream was interpreted as one that included seven years of plenty followed by seven years of famine. Joseph instructed the king to store up a portion of the harvest during the time of plenty so as not to be caught unprepared during the seven years of famine.

CHAPTER 1: OUR CHARACTER

Bringing the story full circle, Joseph's father, Jacob, sent his sons to Egypt to buy grain as they were unprepared and at a point of starvation. Roughly 23 years had passed since his brothers had seen him, so they did not recognize him. However, Joseph recognized his brothers. In such a high position, Joseph could have finally sought revenge on his brothers. He had the power to turn, enslave or even kill them had it been his will. But this man took a totally different route. He forgave them, he embraced them, he fed them, and he loved them.

When I say this was a high-level account of his story, trust me, it was a very high-level account. Joseph's story spanned roughly 23 years. But let's look at the humility this man had! With everything he went through, once he reached a place of power, he never set himself above anyone. Humility, according to the Collins English Dictionary, means modesty, meekness, and submissiveness. Here's what the Scriptures say in Matthew 5:9. "Blessed are the meek: for they shall inherit the earth. Blessed are they which do hunger and thirst after righteousness: for they shall be filled. Blessed are the merciful: for they shall obtain mercy. Blessed are the pure in heart: for they shall see God. Blessed are the peacemakers: for they shall be called the children of God."

Matthew 23:11-12 (NAS) continues with, "But the greatest among you shall be your servant. And whoever exalts himself shall be humbled; and whoever humbles himself shall be exalted."

The characteristic of humility is crucial for spiritual warriors, and they cannot allow pride or boastfulness to have any place in their lives. They must understand that it is not by their power nor their might lest any man should boast. Any victory they gain is only by their submission to the Lord God Almighty. Humility and submission go hand in hand.

James 4:6, 7 says, "But He gives us more grace. This is why it says: "God opposes the proud but gives grace to the humble. Submit yourselves, then, to God. Resist the devil, and he will flee from you."

CHAPTER 1: OUR CHARACTER

4. Passionate

When there is passion in what you are passionate about, you will protect it at any cost...that's a warrior! Being passionate about something means you have an overwhelming urgency to act on whatever that something is. I have always believed the fire that burns deep down within you helps to guide you towards fulfilling your purpose. I love the way Jeremiah 20:9 describes it, "Then I said, I will not make mention of him, nor speak any more in his name. But his word was in mine heart as a burning fire shut up in my bones, and I was weary with forbearing, and I could not stay." In this passage of scripture, the prophet, Jeremiah, was referencing the Word of God that burned deep in his spirit. A word that, because of its disparaging message, he often felt threatened. Here he is stating that he has tried fervently not to speak the Word of God over the people of Judah but try hard as he might, he could not keep silent. The Word of God was burning a fire so deep and so strong within him that he was not able to contain it.

CHAPTER 1: OUR CHARACTER

True prophets of old did not "prophesy feel" good messaged. Quite the contrary, their prophecies were mostly those of gloom and despair. Jeremiah's very mission was to warn the people of Judah about their impending demise if they did not turn away from their wickedness. Can you imagine being out doing your job or something you were obligated to do, but you are met with people who despised you? There are those who resented you and even those who wanted to kill you. Yet, instead of retreating, you had the press in you to continue fulfilling your purpose even in the face of adversity? That's passion! When I think of the word passion, I think of conviction. A person's conviction is a matter in which they have a strong opinion or belief. That conviction, coupled with an urgency inside of them to "do," is how I view passion.

As you can see, having a passion about what you are fighting for in battle will propel you to do all you can do to claim the victory. What I love about fighting spiritual battles is that most times, the best thing we can do is fervently go to God in prayer and praise Him for the victory because He is the one that is fighting for us anyway. We will get into that a little later. But passion is a

CHAPTER 1: OUR CHARACTER

part of a person's character that makes them get out of their seat. It makes them speak up against things that they do not perceive as just. And I love this one; it makes them continue to stand firm and fight even when the odds are against them. This is why it is so vital for a spiritual warrior to have the characteristic of passion.

This is a psalm written by David when he was in the wilderness of Judah. "O God, you are my God; earnestly I seek you; my soul thirsts for you; my flesh faints for you, as in a dry and weary land where there is no water" (Psalm 63:1). Before we go on, I want you to make a declaration over your own life. But be warned, do not do this if you do not truly mean it. Your words carry weight. God needs to hear the passion in this declaration prayer.

"I declare that I am a warrior. I declare that I have the mind of a warrior. I declare that I have the heart of a warrior. I will stay ready and my life will be full of prayer. I will not think of myself more highly than I should, and I will protect what I am passionate about. I seal my declaration with the Holy Spirit and in the name of Jesus, Amen."

CHAPTER 1: OUR CHARACTER

We could go into many characters in the Bible and in our own lives who have the kind of passion that wins wars. But the One who is our greatest example is Jesus Christ. He exemplified every characteristic we have mentioned and so many more! Jesus was always "at the ready." Even at an early age when Mary and John were looking for Him, His words to them were, "I must be about my Father's business."

Jesus was quick to pray—He gave us the greatest outline ever for prayer. In Matthew 6:9-13, we find what has been coined "The Lord's Prayer." Not only did He give us the model for prayer, He was the model for prayer. Jesus was always praying before making any decisions. Prayer was His line to the Father. Prayer is also our line to the Father.

Jesus was humble...the King of Kings and Lord of Lords rode into Jerusalem on a donkey. His trade was that of a carpenter, which was a very lowly profession. His clothes were not flashy, and His presence was not intimidating. Jesus, the Son of the Living God who has all power in His hands, and yet, He did not brag nor did He boast.

CHAPTER 1: OUR CHARACTER

And because He was all of these things and He lives inside each of us, then we too are warriors. We too can learn to be slow to anger and quick to pray. We too can humble ourselves, and we all are passionate about something! Jesus said in John 14:12, "Verily, verily, I say unto you, He that believeth on me, the works that I do shall he do also; and greater works than these shall he do; because I go unto my Father."

CHAPTER 2

OUR TOOLKITS

Now may the God of peace, who through the blood of the eternal covenant brought back from the dead our Lord Jesus, that great Shepherd of the sheep, equip you with everything good for doing his will, and may he work in us what is pleasing to him, through Jesus Christ, to whom be glory for ever and ever. Amen.

Hebrews 13:20-21 (NIV)

CHAPTER 2: OUR TOOLKITS

In Ephesians 6:10-20, the Bible tells us how to defend ourselves as follows, "Finally, be strong in the Lord and in the strength of his might. Put on the whole armor of God that you may be able to stand against the schemes of the devil. For we do not wrestle against flesh and blood, but against the rulers, against the authorities, against the cosmic powers over this present darkness, against the spiritual forces of evil in the heavenly places. Therefore take up the whole armor of God, that you may be able to withstand in the evil day, and having done all, to stand firm. Stand therefore, having fastened on the belt of truth, and having put on the breastplate of righteousness, and, as shoes for your feet, having put on the readiness given by the gospel of peace. In all circumstances take up the shield of faith, with which you can extinguish all the flaming darts of the evil one; and take the helmet of salvation, and the sword of the Spirit, which is the word of God, praying at all times in the

CHAPTER 2: OUR TOOLKITS

Spirit, with all prayer and supplication. To that end, keep alert with all perseverance, making supplication for all the saints, and also for me, that words may be given to me in opening my mouth boldly to proclaim the mystery of the gospel, for which I am an ambassador in chains, that I may declare it boldly, as I ought to speak."

In order to effectively prepare yourself to fight any enemy, natural or spiritual, you have to not only be familiar with the weapons you have on hand. But you also need to know those weapons intimately. You cannot be "sniper ready" if you have no clue how to properly hold a rifle. Yeah, you can figure out how to pull the trigger, but do you have the right posture? Is your target lined up in your sight? Is the safety off? Did you even load the cartridge, and is there a round in the chamber? You can't be a watchman on the wall if you don't know how to operate the gear that enhances your vision. Do you know how to spot an intruder in the dark? Do you know what alarms to sound depending on the situation? Do you know how to use your offensive weapons? We can't just know we have access to our weapons; we must know how to effectively use those

CHAPTER 2: OUR TOOLKITS

weapons. What weapons am I referring to? Because we are fighting a spiritual war, we must focus our attention not on the tangible but on intangible weapons. Clearly, we would never grab a 9mm Glock to shoot a demon. We must set our minds on the things above. Let's walk through some potential weapons of warfare.

Weapon 1: The Word of God

Is it any surprise the most powerful weapon you can use in spiritual warfare is the Word of God? The Book of Divine Inspiration tells you that within its mesmerizing pages as we are putting on our "Whole Armor of God." The single and most powerful offensive weapon we possess is the Word of God. As you see in the Scripture quoted at the beginning of this chapter, our armor is top heavy on items to put us in a defensive stance. Defense is important in a fight for your life; however, when you are ready to go into attack mode, defensive strategies won't help you win. However, when you apply offensive tactics, you are declaring war on your enemy. You are no longer exuding the majority of your energy on fighting off the enemy; you are putting yourself in a position to win against your

CHAPTER 2: OUR TOOLKITS

enemy. Let's explore what the Word says will happen if we put it to work.

"For the word of God is alive and active. Sharper than any double-edged sword, it penetrates even to dividing soul and spirit, joints and marrow; it judges the thoughts and attitudes of the heart" (Hebrews 4:12 [NIV]).

"He that believeth on me, as the scripture hath said, out of his belly shall flow rivers of living water" (John 7:38).

"So shall my word be that goeth forth out of my mouth: it shall not return unto me void, but it shall accomplish that which I please, and it shall prosper in the thing whereto I sent it" (Isaiah 55:11).

"He sent his word, and healed them, and delivered them from their destructions" (Psalm 107:20).

I am reminded of a song we used to sing in church by Donald Lawrence *entitled "One Word Away."* This song speaks directly to this principal. Here is a portion of the lyrics.

CHAPTER 2: OUR TOOLKITS

"One word away! One word away!
The power of life and death is in what you say
Ooooh
One word away! One word away!
If you start confessing,
You will start possessing
The key to your success is a word away!
Let the word do the work. Let the word Let the word
do the work"

With that being said, begin putting this weapon into action. Let the Word do the work in your life. In the Appendix, you will find several scriptures for applying the Word directly to the many situations we encounter in life.

Weapon 2: Praise

What is praise? Praise is an expression of adoration. It is a show of love and admiration for one who is esteemed highly. Praise is an outward expression of an inner feeling. I believe that praise is God's way to keep us humble and refocus our attention from situations and focus on the One who can handle any situation. Understand

CHAPTER 2: OUR TOOLKITS

something; God does not need your approval. He is not trying to get the 'big head' by requiring your praise. What He is doing is grooming you to think less about yourself and more about Him. Have you ever witnessed when children first attempt to walk? The more you praise their success, the more determined they are to do it again. God functions in the same way. The more you praise Him, the more inclined He is to continue to work on your behalf. These are some praises taken directly from the Word of God:

"This people I have formed for Myself; They shall declare My praise (Isaiah 43:21 [NKJV])."

"But you are a chosen people, a royal priesthood, a holy nation, a people for God's own possession, to proclaim the virtues of Him who called you out of darkness into His marvelous light" (1 Peter 2:9).

"Then we, Your people, the sheep of Your pasture, will thank You forever; from generation to generation, we will declare Your praise" (Psalm 79:13).

CHAPTER 2: OUR TOOLKITS

Praise is indeed our expression of love for a God who is our everything. But there is something else that praise does that makes it an offensive weapon for us. I know you may have heard of this before, it the phrase "Praise confuses the enemy!" If you are wondering if this is really scripturally sound, then consider this, as soon as they started shouting and praising, GOD set ambushes against the men of Ammon, Moab, and Mount Seir as they were attacking Judah, and they all ended up dead. The Ammonites and Moabites mistakenly attacked those from Mount Seir and massacred them. Then, further confused, they went at each other, and all ended up killed as told to us in 2 Chronicles 20:22 (Message).

Can you imagine going up against your foe, but before you can even pull out your swords, you see them fighting one another in a confused fury? That's the power of the God we serve! The more we praise Him, especially in our darkest days, the more it confuses those who come up against us. If you remember in the book of Job, his friends told him to curse God and die. But Job continued to whole strong on his convictions and outwardly said, "Though He slay me, yet will I trust Him." Can you see how that would

CHAPTER 2: OUR TOOLKITS

confuse those around you who do not have the same level of faith? We will dive into this a little more in a later chapter but know that when you praise God through EVERYTHING, and I do mean EVERYTHING, you go through in life, He is right there with you. The more you love Him, the more He pours that love right back on you. You are favored, you are loved, and you are protected through your sincere praise.

One last point on praise. Praise comes in so many forms. I am someone who wrestles with chronic vocal dysfunction. I am not claiming it, and it does not define me, but it is something that I have had to fight for much of my life. I learned not to let my inability to speak interrupt my praise. I learned that if I can cry out to God in the natural, I can do it in the spirit. I use my gestures to give Him praise, and I allow my writing to give Him praise. I utilize my clapping, my stomping, my banging on a desk, and even my smile and lifting up of holy hands to give Him praise. No matter what, I will not let a rock praise God in my place. I will not let a donkey praise God in my place. As long as I have breath in my body, voice or no voice, I will praise ye the Lord!

Weapon 3: Prayer

Many of us know that one of our most powerful weapons against the enemy is prayer. Prayer is communication with God. So how does a conversation with God constitute a weapon of warfare? God is Omniscient, He is Omnipotent, and He is Omnipresent...all-knowing, all-powerful, and ever-present. If you are in a war, wouldn't it make sense to confide in your most powerful ally? God gives us dunamis power. He gives us exousia. He is the one who supplies all of our needs. The word tells us that greater is the God who is in me than the god who is in the world. Notice the big 'G' and the little 'g.' Our God is greater, He is bigger, He is more powerful, He is the great I Am! There is no little 'g' god that can compare to our God!

Prayer can be extremely powerful if used in the correct manner. I am not saying that there is a right or wrong way to pray. Jesus gave us the greatest example of prayer in Matthews 6:5-15. So, the blueprints for prayer are already laid out for you. But when we are praying as it relates to spiritual warfare, we have to be intentional, we have to be bold, and we have to be direct. It's not just enough to recite what is affectionally known as "The Lord's Prayer." We must understand how to break it down. How to interpret it and how to use it in warfare. Open your Bible to Matthew 6:5-15 and let's break it down.

Our Father = This gives an identity to the relationship we have with God. He is not just an unfamiliar deity, but He has a relationship with us and us with Him. It goes beyond just saying God because there are many gods in the world, but Our Father indicates our relationship with Him. If we view God as Our Father…we view Him as our head, our protector, our caregiver, our provider. Feel free to insert any other attributes that you would associate with a loving father. Wouldn't you much rather have a loving father by your side fighting with and for you?

Which art in heaven = Identifies God's position. It establishes His governmental authority and his supremacy. We worship the God of the heavens and of the earth! He has ALL POWER in His possession. When we go into warfare prayer, we need to connect with the One who we know is the Great I Am. My pastor, John Das of Revive

CHAPTER 2: OUR TOOLKITS

Church in Charlotte, North Carolina, preached a series on Spiritual Warfare, and one of his topics was 'Battle Buddies'. These are the people we choose to war with and the ones we trust to have our backs. They are the ones who understand the war we are fighting. Who is a better Battle Buddy to have on your side than God Himself?

Hallowed be thy name = Merriam Webster defines hallowed as holy, consecrated; sacred, revered. We just talked about the importance of praise. As it relates to our warfare prayer, praising God in this manner establishes that we put no other god before Him. This releases us to submit ourselves to God. If we acknowledge our reverence for Him, and Him alone, it puts our enemy on alert that we know who we are and we know whose we are!

Thy kingdom come = As God has established His reign in heaven, we should also want His same reign here on earth. One of the many things I love about God is that He has ultimate supremacy, and yet He does not force Himself on any of us. Instead, He waits for us to welcome Him in.

CHAPTER 2: OUR TOOLKITS

Thy will be done in earth, as it is in heaven = When we are warring, we cannot lean on our own understanding. Sometimes we get caught up as humans and begin wanting our own agendas to be done. But here, we are taught that it has to be God's will that is done. If our will does not align with His will, then we must certainly focus on His will. God is our Creator. The things He created in heaven are what we want to be manifested here on earth. This is a big part of declaring and decreeing. We want to declare God's will on earth and declare God's power on the earth. Declaring invites God into your situation. Decreeing positions God to set the same establishments that are in heaven to be so on the earth. Isn't it amazing to know God has established health for you? He has established victory for you. He has established blessings for you. He has established peace for you. Decree those things into your life as God has already manifested them in the heavenly realms.

Give us this day our daily bread = As we are fighting whatever enemy we are fighting, we must always seek God for provision for each day, not for purposes of greed. We need Him to provide what we need so our focus is not on those needs but on the battle. This also speaks to our humanity and level of humility. We often say, "I got this" or "I got me," but in reality, we need to humble ourselves and understand God can be the only one who has us. He is the source of every resource we need here on earth. Yes, we should make provision for our futures and the futures of our families, but when you are warring, you can only take into battle those things that you need for the day, believing that God will give us victory and the resources we need for the next day and the next day.

And forgive us our debts as we forgive our debtors = We cannot go into battle without first checking our mess at the door. Just like above, we do not want to carry additional baggage with us as we prepare for war. We have to have love, peace, and humility in our hearts as we move forward in battle. We must first ask God for forgiveness and repent (turn away) from anything that we have done out of the will of God. Then, we have to forgive those who have wronged us and receive forgiveness from those we have wronged. Just as important, we must learn how to forgive ourselves. Many Christians get hung up in the concept of forgiving others but do not believe that they

CHAPTER 2: OUR TOOLKITS

can also forgive themselves. This is a practice that will set many a captive free! Remember, ask God for forgiveness, forgive others, receive forgiveness from others and forgive yourself! It is time to check our pride at the door. Unforgiveness, whether not given or not received, can be a yoke (bondage) around our necks that can cause us to lose the war. And if we do not forgive others, how can we expect God to forgive us? And as it is written in the scriptures:

"For if ye forgive men their trespasses, your heavenly Father will also forgive you: But if ye forgive not men their trespasses, neither will your Father forgive your trespasses" (Matt. 6:14-15).

And lead us not into temptation but deliver us from evil = It is important to note that as we are engaged in spiritual warfare, one of the biggest tricks the devil will use is temptation. We have to ask God to help us resist temptation (resist the devil). In the same vein, when we are in the presence of evil, it can be overwhelming if we are not prepared in advance. This part of the prayer is for God's covering over us.

CHAPTER 2: OUR TOOLKITS

For thine is the kingdom, and the power, and the glory, forever. Amen = As we began with worshipping and praising Our Father...so must we end our prayers. This solidifies that we have not lost focus and that we know that he is our beginning and our end.

Now that we have examined this prayer in depth, here are a few additional prayers that cover various areas of your life and follow the format of the Lord's Prayer. Let's pray...

General Warfare

Holy and everlasting Father, we come before You in earnest reverence. Acknowledging Your sovereignty and power. Lord, we ask that You forgive us for any trespasses against any man and especially against You, and we receive forgiveness from all who have wronged us. We also ask that you teach us how to forgive ourselves. Just as You cast our trespasses in the sea of forgetfulness when we come to You, we also ask that You open that sea for us to forgive ourselves. We repent before You, God, and ask that You would grant us

CHAPTER 2: OUR TOOLKITS

a clean slate as we desire to live the life that You have predestined for us. Father, we come before You and declare victory on the earth as it already is so in heaven. For though we live in this world, we do not wage war as this world wages war. The weapons we fight with are not carnal. They are mighty and have divine power to demolish strongholds. So, as we come to You, Lord God, we declare a demolishing of arguments and everything that sets itself up against the knowledge of You, and we take captive every thought to make it obedient to You! We recognize that it is not by our power or our strength but by Your Spirit, Lord, that we seek victory. We walk in the exousia that only You have given us. We cast down imaginations and every high thing that exalts itself against the knowledge of God and bring into captivity every thought to the obedience of Christ. Father God, we thank You in advance for the wonderful works of Your hands. We glorify You for being Abba Father and for loving us as only You can. We humble ourselves before You as we seek Your face in all that we do. We honor and adore You, in Jesus' name we pray. Amen.

Deliverance

Glorious and merciful God, we honor Your Holy and righteous name. El-Shaddai, there is none on earth like You and known in heaven but You! We thank You for Your gentle mercy, and we come before You with repentance in our hearts. We ask that You would forgive us for the wrongs done in our feeble humanity, and we seek Your mercy and grace as we turn away from all manner of evil. Lord, we come before You with the dunamis power granted to us by You as we tread on serpents and scorpions and over all the power of the enemy. We decree a binding on earth as it is in heaven, and a loosing on earth as it is in heaven. We acknowledge that in all things, we are more than conquerors because of Your love and grace over our lives. Lord, we declare that Your Word going forth from our mouths will not return unto You void but will accomplish all that You have set forth for it to accomplish and that it shall prosper in the

CHAPTER 2: OUR TOOLKITS

things where forth You have sent it. May Your Word flow out of our belly as rivers of living water. May they heal the sick, mend the hearts of the broken, and restore faith to those who have lost hope. We know that the devil prowls around like a roaring lion seeking whom he may destroy, but with the boldness given to us by You, we resist his advances. We place him under our feet, and we cast him back to the pits of hell where he belongs. Where our enemy tries to come against us one way...we decree that he flee before us seven ways. We speak Your Word as our foundation of faith. We stand firmly on the rock, which is You, the rock where You built Your church, God, that the gates of hell shall not prevail against us! We give the battle to You, Our Protector, as we dwell in the shelter of You, Most High. We will rest and abide in Your shadow. We acknowledge You as our fortress in whom we trust. We give thanks to You, Father, who gives us victory through our Lord Jesus Christ. We bow in Your presence, O God, and sing Your praises from everlasting to everlasting. In Jesus' name we humbly submit to You and seal this prayer. Amen.

Provision

Jehovah Jireh, we bless Your name on high! We magnify and glorify You. Lord, we seek Your face in the pardoning of our sins and Your shelter as our refuge. We acknowledge Your sovereignty as we yield our needs to You. Lord, we pray for an overflow of financial peace and security to overtake us, our household, our family, and our friends. We seek Your provision now more than ever. As You fed the birds of the air who neither sow nor reap nor gather into barns; yet will You feed us. As You have clothed the lilies of the fields, we trust that You will also clothe us. Lord, we put all of our needs and all of our cares before You, and we lay them at Your feet. We seek You first and Your righteousness, and we believe that those things we stand in need of You will provide. We thank You for being a God of provision. We give you unbridled adoration as we yield ourselves to You. In the precious name of Jesus, Amen.

CHAPTER 2: OUR TOOLKITS

Healing

Jehovah Rapha, we surrender to You. We acknowledge You as our divine healer. We marvel at the works of Your hands. Lord, we call upon Your healing virtue to penetrate any manner of sickness that befalls us. We cry out to You to send Your healing angels by our bedside. We decree Your healing virtues to penetrate our bodies from the crown of our heads to the souls of our feet. We call every cell, artery, vein, and organ to come under subjection to You as it was You who designed our bodies to function in an intricate way. We plead the blood of Jesus over our bodies as we submit them as living sacrifices holy and acceptable to You. Lord, we declare that as You were wounded for our transgressions, bruised for our iniquities; and bore the chastisement for our peace, that Your stripes continue to heal us. We are but one body and one spirit. Just as You were called in one hope of Your calling, You are our Lord and God. You are Father of all, above all, through all and in You is all. We honor You, in Jesus' name, Amen.

CHAPTER 2: OUR TOOLKITS

Peace

Hallelujah! God, we give You the highest praise! We lift up our voices in total adoration unto You. We reverence You in the beauty of Your holiness! We call upon You now, Jehovah Shalom, God of our peace. That You would still our hearts and our minds. That You would give us a sense of serenity in the midst of the chaos that is all around us. We look to the hills from which cometh our help, knowing our help comes from You. It is You who have made us and not we ourselves. You have planted Your peace within us that no weapon that forms against us will prosper. We will not subject ourselves to the chaos that tries to engulf us, for You did not give us the spirit of fear but of power, of love, and of a sound mind. Continue to provide us with the peace that surpasses understanding. Guard our hearts and our minds as You incline our ears to You. Teach us to lay aside every weight that hinders us and console those of us who mourn. Give us beauty for ashes, the oil of joy for mourning, and the garment of praise for the spirit of heaviness; that we may be called trees of righteousness. And that You may be glorified. With every breath that's in us, we praise Your Holy and Righteous name. in Jesus' name we pray, Amen.

Repentance and Salvation

Our God, who art in heaven, hallowed would be thy name. Thy kingdom come; thy will be done on earth as it is in heaven. Father, we humbly bow before You asking that You would forgive us of any sin that separates us from the love of You. We ask that You purge us with hyssop, that we shall be clean: wash us, and we shall be whiter than snow. Lord, make us to hear joy and gladness; that the bones which thou hast broken may rejoice. Hide thy face from our sins and blot out all of our iniquities. Create in us a clean heart, O God, and renew a right spirit within us. Cast us not away from Thy presence and take not Thy Holy Spirit from us. Restore unto us the joy of our salvation and uphold us with Thy free spirit. Lead us down Roman's Road where we understand that all have sinned and fallen short of the glory of God. We

CHAPTER 2: OUR TOOLKITS

acknowledge that the wages of sin is death, but the free gift of God is eternal life in Christ Jesus our Lord. As You have shown Your love for us in that while we were still sinners, You sent Your son Jesus to die for us. So, we confess with our mouths that Jesus is Lord and believe in our hearts that God raised Him from the dead, Save us, O God. For with the heart, one believes and is justified, and with the mouth, one confesses and is saved. Therefore, since we have been justified by faith, we have peace with God through our Lord Jesus Christ.

Praise

Who is this King of glory? The Lord strong and mighty, the Lord mighty in battle. Lift up your heads, O ye gates; even lift them up, ye everlasting doors; and the King of glory shall come in. Who is this King of glory? The Lord of hosts, He is the King of glory. God, we come before you not to ask of anything from You but to give our best offering of praise to You. We sing HALLELUJAH, which is the highest praise, to Your name. We magnify You,

CHAPTER 2: OUR TOOLKITS

God, with all that is within us. We shabach Your name in a voice of triumph. We adore You, God, as a wife adores her husband and as an infant adores his mother. We speak of Your goodness and Your mercy everywhere we go, and we acknowledge You as Jehovah Tsidkenu, the God of our righteousness. Lord, You are our God; we will exalt You and praise Your name, for in perfect faithfulness, You have done wonderful things. Our hearts leap for joy, and with our song, we praise You! Because Your love is better than life, our lips will glorify You. We will praise You as long as we live, and in Your name, we will lift up our hands. We shall praise You, Lord, of our souls; and all that is within us, we shall bless Your holy name. So let everything that has breath praise the Lord, praise ye the Lord! In Jesus' name we pray, Amen.

Faith

Our Father, which art in heaven, hallowed would be thy name. You are our rock and our strong tower. We take comfort in knowing that under Your shield of protection we can hide and not be

CHAPTER 2: OUR TOOLKITS

afraid. We sing Holy Holy Holy unto You O' God. We ask that Your divine will be done here on earth as it is in heaven. Those things that You have for us, may they be released in the name of Jesus. Merciful God, we pray that You would increase our faith. We pray that You would give to us a double measure of faith, Lord. We stand on Your word that whosoever shall say unto this mountain, be thou removed, and be thou cast into the sea; and shall not doubt in his heart, but shall believe that those things which he saith shall come to pass; he shall have whatsoever he saith. We are speaking to the mountains in our lives Lord. We are casting down every and every high thing that exalteth itself against the knowledge of You, and bringing into captivity every thought to the obedience of You Christ. I desire the faith as a mustard seed Lord so that I can grow in my convictions. I stand on faith, believing that every valley shall be filled, and by faith, every mountain and hill shall be brought low. By faith, I believe the crooked places in my life shall be made straight, and the rough ways shall be made smooth. Thank you that Your word shall not return unto You void but shall accomplish everything You have set forth for it to accomplish! By faith I decree that it is so, in Jesus' name, Amen.

Blessings

Mighty God, I give You my sacrifice of praise. I praise You from the rising of the sun to the going down of the same. I sing praises unto thee and I shall honor thee all the days of my life. I thank You Lord that You allow me to freely come to you to repent of my sins and my transgressions. Lord forgive me for those things I have done that do not align with Your word. If there is anything that I have done knowingly or not to You or any of Your children, I humbly come to You and seek Your forgiveness. I thank You that You do not keep record of wrong but that You take those sins and cast them into the sea of forgetfulness. I come to You praying for blessings over me and my family Lord. I pray Deuteronomy 28 blessings over us God, that we may be blessed in the city, and blessed in the field. I pray that our fruit shall be blessed. I pray that blessed shall be our basket and our store. Blessed we will be when we comest in, and blessed shalt we be when we go out. I ask that You would cause our enemies that rise up against us to be smitten before our faces. That they shall come out against us one way, and flee before us seven ways. Lord I declare blessings upon our storehouses, and in all that we set our hands to do. I decree; blessings in the land which You have giveth us. Lord, we trust that You shall establish us as a holy people unto You. Lord I pray that all people of the earth shall see that we art called by Your name and they shall be afraid of You. I declare that you would make us plenteous in goods, in the fruit of our body, and in the fruit of all that you swore unto our fathers to give to us. By faith we know that You shall open unto us your good treasure, You shall bless all the work of our hands. As it is in heaven, I decree on earth that we shall be lenders and not borrows. We shall be the head and not the tail and we shall be above and not beneath. We seal this prayer as we give Your name continuous praise, in Jesus' name, Amen.

Weapon 4: Fruit of the Spirit

"But the fruit of the Spirit is love, joy, peace, forbearance, kindness, goodness, faithfulness, gentleness and self-control. Against such things there is no law" (Galatians 5:22-23 [NIV]).

The surprise attack weapon I would like to introduce to your arsenal is the Fruit of the Spirit. I know you are wondering how this could possibly be a part of your warfare arsenal. How can love, joy, peace, longsuffering, gentleness, goodness, faith, meekness, and temperance help us win a battle? Collectively, these attributes are important because they strengthen a very important muscle in battle – Self Control. You cannot go into war and expect to win if you are fighting out of blind rage or blind fury.

The scripture tells us in Ephesians 4:26-32, "Be angry and do not sin; do not let the sun go down on your anger and give no opportunity to the devil. Let the thief no longer steal, but rather let him labor, doing honest work with his own hands, so that he may have something to

CHAPTER 2: OUR TOOLKITS

share with anyone in need. Let no corrupting talk come out of your mouths, but only such as is good for building up, as fits the occasion, that it may give grace to those who hear. And do not grieve the Holy Spirit of God, by whom you were sealed for the day of redemption. Let all bitterness and wrath and anger and clamor and slander be put away from you, along with all malice. Be kind to one another, tenderhearted, forgiving one another, as God in Christ forgave you."

This may not sound like a weapon, but I assure you, if you practice self-control and strengthen that muscle, victory shall be yours. It is ok to be angry, but sin not. In other words, it is ok to have the passion and the drive to fight when necessary but don't let that anger overtake you. Don't let it make you lose sight of your enemy and his tricks. Don't allow your enemy to control your movements because he has put you in a blind fight or flight position. When offense comes knocking at your door, and the enemy challenges you to war, self-control will allow you to focus, it will allow you to be proactive, not reactive, and it will allow you to strategize with a clear head. If you lose self-control, it is so much harder to think through logical strategies.

Another very important purpose of the Fruit of the Spirit weapon is that it can be used to confuse the enemy. Every battle that comes your way doesn't need to be fought in the natural. Yes, I know that in the Old Testament, there were many instances where physical wars were fought. But thank God, most of us don't have to fight from a physical perspective. However, we all endure spiritual battles on a regular basis. This book is intended to help you fight spiritual warfare.

Weapon 5: Faith

"But without faith it is impossible to please him: for he that cometh to God must believe that he is, and that he is a rewarder of them that diligently seek him" (Hebrews 11:6).

Not sure much more needs to be said but let me see what's in my spiritual chambers about faith. Faith is the foundation of our belief as Christians. Faith is believing in

CHAPTER 2: OUR TOOLKITS

the unseen. Faith is trusting a God who you cannot see to move on your behalf in situations that you can see. Faith is unwavering love. Faith makes the intangible tangible. I could go on and on. Faith has such profound power. I love how the Bible tells us that we are a peculiar people. Part of this peculiarity is that we believe in a power that is well beyond our reach. I guess people who do not yet know God would find our actions and beliefs to be a bit off. But we know a God who can do anything and everything but fail! As it pertains to spiritual warfare, as Ephesians 6 tells us, faith is our shield. It is the defensive weapon that we use to protect all areas of our lives. It guards us against the fiery darts of the enemy. It amazes me how people exercise a level of faith in inanimate objects every single day, yet when we talk about faith in God Himself, they question our sanity. We can trust that an airplane will remain in the sky when we travel, we trust that a chair will handle our weight, and we even trust that our bodies will intake and excrete those things that it should, but we fight when it comes to believing in a God that makes all these things possible.

CHAPTER 3

STRATEGY

By wisdom a house is built, and by understanding it is established; by knowledge the rooms are filled with all precious and pleasant riches.

Proverbs 24:3-4

CHAPTER 3: STRATEGY

The best way to defeat the enemy is to understand him and how he fights. Not only do you have to have your own plan of attack when going into battle, but you must also study your opponent. Something I grew up hearing was the best way to win against an opponent is to study his moves. If you know his style of fighting, his "go-to" moves, and his mental strategies for war, then you can plan your strategy in a way that combats his moves and shakes him up. When you watch fighters in a wrestling match, you notice that if they truly know their opponent, they know their "signature" moves. So, to not get taken down by these signature moves, you create a counterattack, a plan of escape. If I know someone is going into a stance to put me in a headlock, I am going to position my body to break that hold.

In the movie *The Usual Suspects* (Bryan Singer, 1995), Kevin Spacey's character makes a very profound

CHAPTER 3: STRATEGY

statement. He said, "The greatest trick the devil ever pulled was convincing the world he didn't exist." This is why it is so important to study your enemy. If you do not believe he exists, you do not believe him to be a threat. Yet the Bible tells us that satan comes to steal, to kill, and to destroy. He is real, and the sooner we accept that, the better we can prepare ourselves against him. We know that he doesn't have new tricks; he continues to regurgitate the same old types of attacks. Mind you, he may try in a different way, but the attack itself is the same. For example, if alcohol is a weakness for you, no matter how long you celebrate sobriety, satan is going to continue to tempt you with alcohol. He may try to entice you at a party, persuade you at a work gala, or peer pressure you when you are out with your friends. If you are already aware of this attack, you expect it. When you expect it, you can plan your counter in advance.

Another example can be fornication. If you know that your desire for the opposite sex is strong and a major weakness for you. Satan is going to attack you by putting the well-built, good-smelling man in your path that will cause you to lose your mind. Or he will sashay that gorgeous full-

CHAPTER 3: STRATEGY

bodied woman with that million-dollar smile in your face and watch you drool until you give in. But if you are already aware of these tricks, you can build yourself in your most holy faith to come against these temptations. You can pray that you will be strong, you can find an escape route when needed, and you can gain victory when the enemy wants so badly to see you defeated. The greatest part of your strategy is to understand his!

But let's not spend so much time studying his moves that we don't master our own moves. Countering satan's moves is great, but if you don't have a signature move of your own, you will constantly be on the defensive. We know that defense is key in a football game, but it is the offensive team's point scoring that wins the game. It's great to resist the devil, but we also want to level up and be victorious! The Word tells us that we are more than conquerors. A conqueror subdues and overcomes an opponent and wins the victory. But we are MORE THAN CONQUERORS. We don't just win one battle. As Christians, we win in the present tense, which means we keep on winning! Every day we have breath in our body;

CHAPTER 3: STRATEGY

we also have a win in our spirit! Sit on that for a minute, and then praise your way through.

CHAPTER 4

BATTLE READY

For you equipped me with strength for the battle; you made those who rise against me sink under me.

Psalm 18:39

CHAPTER 4: BATTLE READY

"Submit yourselves therefore to God. Resist the devil, and he will flee from you." James 4:7

"So, let God work his will in you. Yell a loud no to the Devil and watch him make himself scarce. Say a quiet yes to God and he'll be there in no time. Quit dabbling in sin. Purify your inner life. Quit playing the field. Hit bottom and cry your eyes out. The fun and games are over. Get serious, really serious. Get down on your knees before the Master; it's the only way you'll get on your feet." James 4:7-10 (MSG)

So, what is Battle Ready? Cambridge dictionary defines it as being sufficiently equipped, trained, and numerically strong to engage an enemy. To be battle-ready means that we have counted the cost, we have not just put on the full armor of God, but we have also trained ourselves in how to use it.

CHAPTER 4: BATTLE READY

To be battle ready means we are COVERED. Everything that God wants to give us must be ON US, but it must also be IN US. It cannot be something we just talk about but rather something we put into practice.

"For you equipped me with strength for the battle; you made those who rise against me sink under me" (Psalms 18:39).

As Christians, we face battles against our enemy, satan, and all powers of darkness. He is constantly throwing fiery darts, and they aim for our most vulnerable areas (our marriages, our finances, our health, our mental stability, our relationships). We no sooner defend ourselves against one dart attack before another comes straight for our heads. Sometimes, it feels as if we are defending ourselves against multiple fiery darts at once.

Let me add this caveat: People ARE NOT our enemy but make no mistake, there is a spirit (good or bad) behind every person. And when that spirit is bad...it becomes our adversary.

CHAPTER 4: BATTLE READY

"For we do not wrestle against flesh and blood, but against principalities, against powers, against the rulers of the darkness of this age, against spiritual hosts of wickedness in the heavenly places" (Ephesians 6:12).

Often, believers will make light of the devil, but let's not get it twisted...he will KILL YOU if you give him the chance. Remember, he is here to steal, kill and destroy. We must take measures to ready ourselves to war! We can either take the "L," or we can prepare ourselves to fight back. Even though we know that the battles we face are spiritual, they look natural, they sound natural, they taste natural, they smell natural, and they most certainly feel natural!

Because of the natural aspect, there is a natural preparation that must be done even before the battle begins.

When I say we need to be Battle Ready, I am saying we need to strengthen both our natural selves and our spiritual selves.

From a natural perspective—Take care of your body because it is the temple of God.

Guard what we call your gates – the things we allow into our gates can directly affect the spiritual condition of our hearts. Specifically, you should guard what you watch, what you listen to, who you touch and who you allow to touch you as well as where you go, what you smell and what you say, taste, or ingest.

- ❖ Be aware of those who are in your circle
- ❖ Stop comparing yourselves to your neighbors
- ❖ Live within your means
- ❖ Tithe – a biblical principle that yields a natural result

From a spiritual perspective, ask yourself this— Because there is also a spiritual aspect to warfare, there is spiritual preparation that must also be done.

- ❖ What are you releasing into the atmosphere?
- ❖ What are you inviting into the atmosphere?
- ❖ What are we entertaining in your thoughts?

CHAPTER 4: BATTLE READY

- ❖ Who do you represent?
- ❖ Who or what is your object of worship?

So spiritually, we need to put our big boy or big girl underwear on and go to war. We need to stop being religious punks and become spiritual warriors! We have been given the authority to speak directly to those demons and demonic forces that are attacking us! Don't just let them take up residence and bring all their friends with them. You are in the fight of your life...breathe life into your fight! Command your morning, declare God's protection over you and those you love, and decree those demons out of your life! God is not looking for passive Outer Court Christians! He is looking for those people who would dare to meet Him in the Holy of Holies and fight!

Let me share this! Not only do we want to make the devil angry, but we also want to infuriate him. I know you think I have truly lost my mind at this point. But when we make the devil that angry, we are also making the Lord pleased. As you are reading this, I hope your faith is leveled up. I pray that your understanding is on a different

CHAPTER 4: BATTLE READY

stratosphere, and I decree that you be not afraid! Remember earlier when I said we want to confuse the enemy? When your enemy becomes blind-rage angry, he becomes frantic, he spins out, he loses control, he becomes confused, and he begins to attack anything that is around him. Usually, that is his own imps and demons. He is weakened to a point where he moves in confusion – and in that weakness, we can find our victory! Let's look at some important aspects of being battle ready.

1. *War Paint*

Covering, Concealment, and Camouflage

In the military, war paint (also known as camouflage paint) is used to hide yourself and your equipment from the enemy. When we are invisible to our enemy, then we can prepare ourselves and even make a sneak attack as warranted. War paint serves three main purposes:

Covering-The term cover is something that provides physical shelter or protection that is sought by people in danger

Concealment-The term concealment refers to something that acts as a hiding place

Camouflage-The act, means, or result of obscuring things to deceive an enemy

Exodus 12:12-13 says, "For I will pass through the land of Egypt that night, and I will strike all the firstborn in the land of Egypt, both man and beast; and on all the gods of Egypt I will execute judgments: I am the LORD. The blood shall be a sign for you, on the houses where you are. And when I see the blood, I will pass over you, and no plague will befall you to destroy you, when I strike the land of Egypt."

In this scripture, we see the blood of an innocent sacrificed lamb was placed over the doorpost of all that believed. This blood (war paint) covering was a sign that God would pass over these homes and spare those that were within its covering. What an amazing example of the covering through the use of innocent blood.

CHAPTER 4: BATTLE READY

But that's not the only example of the concept of war paint. In John 8:1-11, we find the story of a woman who was being accused of adultery. Her accusers were set to stone her to death. But Jesus was present, and He stood as a barrier between the accusers and the accused. He symbolically was her war paint as He covered her, He concealed her, and He camouflaged her. He protected her from the impending harm that was coming her way. But not only did He protect her, but He also forgave her. He confronted her assailants and asked a simple question, "He who is without sin, let him cast the first stone." None of us are sin free...we all are facing our own demons. So, Jesus was able to camouflage her sins by redirecting the men's attention to their own transgressions.

Praise Him, even today, the blood of Jesus is our war paint; Jesus Himself is our war paint. When you accept Christ as your Lord and Savior (submit to God), the blood of Jesus protects you from your enemy! And He is sitting on the right hand of the Father making intercession for us!

2. *War Stance*

The Art of Posturing

When I think about a war stance, the first thing that always comes to my mind is the postures of prayer. We wave our hands in praise, we bow our heads in reverence, we lift both hands and our heads towards God in surrender, we lay prostrate before the Lord in adoration, and the list goes on and on. I do agree that these prayer stances truly have an important role in spiritual warfare and serve a practical place in our everyday communication with God. But I want to share a few other postures that may not come to mind as quickly but are just as important.

Proverbs 4:23 NLT tells us, "Guard your heart above all else, for it determines the course of your life."

Posture of your Heart—The battles we face daily begin with the heart. The enemy knows full well the importance of attacking our hearts to get us to believe something that is not truth. Once we believe in our heart that something is a certain way, we convince our mind to take action, and

CHAPTER 4: BATTLE READY

our soul becomes overwhelmed with that action. I think of the story of Solomon (1 Kings 3:16-28). This is such a powerful show of how the posture of your heart can change the outcome of a situation. To summarize, there were two prostitutes who went before King Solomon. They shared a home. One woman had a baby boy, and three days later, the other woman also had a son. The latter woman's son died during the night because she laid on him. Realizing what she had done, she got up in the middle of the night and took the baby of the first woman and laid her deceased baby beside her instead. When they arose, and the first woman realized what had happened, she confronted the latter, who immediately denied the accusation. Now in the presence of the King, the first woman shared her version of what happened, which the latter denied once again. King Solomon decided that since they could not agree on to whom the child really belonged, he would split the living baby in half and give each woman a half. Immediately, the woman who was the true mother pleaded with the King not to kill this child but instead give him to the woman who was not the mother simply to spare his life. However, the deceitful mother said no, kill the child.

Then the king replied, "Give the first woman the living child, and by no means kill him. She is his mother." When all Israel heard about the judgment which the king had handed down, they feared the king, because they saw that the wisdom of God was in him to administer justice. 1 Kings 3:27)

When our heart attitude is right towards God, we become vessels for His Glory. This woman not only spared the life of her child but the attitude of her heart allowed her to gain victory over her foe.

Posture of Surrender – How can surrender possibly be a victory posture? That is an easy one. It's not the surrender that gives you victory, it is the one to who you surrender that determines your victory. Submitting ourselves to God is the main ingredient in any victory we will ever have over our enemies. We have covered it in previous chapters, God is the great I Am. He is the ultimate source of everything we need and the answer for every battle we face. Romans 12:1-2 says, "Therefore, I urge you, brothers and sisters, in view of God's mercy, to offer your bodies as a living sacrifice, holy and pleasing to God—this is your true and proper worship. Do not conform to the pattern of this world, but be transformed by the renewing of your mind. Then you will be able to test and approve what God's will is—his good, pleasing, and perfect will."

Posture of Boldness – As God gives us His power and authority, there should be a boldness displayed when using it. If we have all of the artillery and training we could ever need to fight a war but lack the confidence in how to use it, we have already lost. It is impossible to convince your enemy you are in control when you cannot convince yourself. Our elders would say you have to have a Holy Ghost boldness. I've repeated it countless times in my walk with Christ, but it has not truly dawned on me what the real meaning of this is until now. Holy Ghost boldness is a boldness where you are not standing on your own, but you are standing in the shadow of the Almighty. You are surrendered, yet you are in control. Holy Ghost boldness is leaning on the Holy Spirit to move you above anything you could have done on your own. It's that, you know that you know that you know kind of belief. Have you noticed whenever you have true knowledge of something, you are not afraid to speak on that thing? As a matter of fact, you speak with a fire, a desire, and a determination. Spiritual boldness comes when you have such a close, strong relationship with God that you know who He is, you know who you are in Him, and you know you have a host of angels fighting alongside you.

Proverbs 28:1 "The wicked flee when no one pursues, but the righteous are like a lion."

Psalm 27:1 "The Lord is my light and my salvation. Whom shall I fear? The Lord is the stronghold of my life, of whom shall I be afraid?"

Posture of Obedience – When you seek God, you must make up your mind to obey whatever He says. Sometimes God will ask us to do things that will not make logical sense. But we serve a supernatural God, so why would we use our fallible logic? If God says to do a thing, then do that thing.

Isaiah 55: 8-9 tells us, "For My thoughts are not your thoughts, neither are your ways My ways, declares the LORD. "For as the heavens are higher than the earth, so

CHAPTER 4: BATTLE READY

My ways are higher than your ways and My thoughts than your thoughts."

God knows things that we do not know. He wants to see our faith in Him even if we are not able to see the outcome for ourselves. While our feeble minds think we are struggling and fighting alone, God knows that His angels are already battle ready. He knows that as soon as one of His children here on earth begins to pray and fast (because some demons only come out through prayer and fasting), His army of angels are activated! Angels stand at the throne of God, waiting to do His bidding, and when we call upon the name of the Lord, God dispatches them to fight on our behalf or work out a need that we have. We have not because we ask not! When Daniel was praying, an answer to his prayer was delayed for 21 days by an evil supernatural being. So, what did Daniel do? He prayed and fasted! The archangel, Michael, had to come to help him defeat the demon. Our prayers activate God's army.

2 Chronicles 20:15: "Thus saith the Lord unto you: 'Be not afraid nor dismayed by reason of this great multitude; for *the battle is not yours*, but God's."

CHAPTER 4: BATTLE READY

Exodus 14:14 (NLT): "The LORD himself will fight for you. Just stay calm."

2 Kings 6:16-17 (NLT): "When the servant of the man of God got up early the next morning and went outside, there were troops, horses, and chariots everywhere. 'Oh, sir, what will we do now?' the young man cried to Elisha. 'Don't be afraid!' Elisha told him. 'For there are more on our side than on theirs!' Then Elisha prayed, 'O LORD, open his eyes and let him see!' The LORD opened the young man's eyes, and when he looked up, he saw that the hillside around Elisha was filled with horses and chariots of fire."

Can you imagine thinking that you are fighting a battle by yourself, but then in the distance, you begin to hear a rumbling and as you turn to see what the noise could be, you see a multitude of angels, beautiful glorious angels, coming up behind you, ready to go into battle with you? Hallelujah! Just another confirmation that the battle is already won. God just needs you to show up! All He needs is your yes!

3. *War Cry*
Prayer, Praise, Cry Out

Isaiah 8:9: "Raise the war cry, you nations, and be shattered! Listen, all you distant lands. Prepare for battle, and be shattered! Prepare for battle, and be shattered!"

Isaiah 42:13: "The Lord will march out like a champion, like a warrior he will stir up his zeal; with a shout he will raise the battle cry and will triumph over his enemies."

We already discussed the power that comes with praising God. When we think about a war cry, we should think about that power on steroids.

Psalms 98:4-6: "Make a joyful noise unto the Lord, all the earth: make a loud noise, and rejoice, and sing praise. Sing unto the LORD with the harp; with the harp, and the voice of a psalm. -With trumpets and sound of cornet make a joyful noise before the LORD, the King."

What does it mean to "make a joyful noise" before the Lord? The Hebrew word is patsach (pawt-sah). This word

CHAPTER 4: BATTLE READY

is not associated with anything quiet or passive. In fact, it indicated a sound so loud that it would split the ears. It meant making a loud noise before an army went into battle and before it engaged an enemy. In Psalms, we may think of shouting joyfully as being similar to a polite worship service. But, in fact, the Bible describes something more like a battle cry. It should have the same kind of intensity associated with going to war. It means praising God with the kind of steadfast, unmovable boldness the Israelites had as they marched around Jericho. It means beseeching God to send not just any angels but His warring angels to fight on your behalf!

If you believe in the power of the resurrection and that Jesus sits on the right hand of God, making intercession for us. If you believe that God is all-powerful and is fighting for you no matter what battle you face. If you believe that no matter what it looks like, the devils and demons in your life are already defeated (financial struggle, marital issues, all manner of sickness, depression, loneliness, whatever you are facing), then there should be a war cry deep inside of you.

CHAPTER 4: BATTLE READY

Understand that my fight may not be your fight, and your fight may not be my fight, but we are all ultimately fighting the same battle! He's the same God we are believing. He has the same power we are receiving, and it is the same devil we are defeating. With this newfound understanding, you should be ready to give your loudest war cry possible to gain your strongest victory! God has placed everything you need inside of you to fight any foe that comes your way. It is now up to you to gain the understanding of how to use what you already have and the faith and boldness to know that no devil in hell can stand against our Almighty God. It is at the name of Jesus that every knee shall bow and every tongue shall confess!

CHAPTER 5

REFUELING

*But they who wait for the L*ORD *shall renew their strength; they shall mount up with wings like eagles; they shall run and not be weary; they shall walk and not faint. For you equipped me with strength for the battle; you made those who rise against me sink under me.*

Isaiah 40:31 (ESV)

CHAPTER 5: REFUELING

Empty Cups Must be Refilled–Spiritual warfare can be exhausting. In this book, I have provided you with a great deal of content that helps you pour all you have onto the Lord and into His work. While emptying out your cup is extremely important. It is equally important to refill it with the rivers of living water. After you pour out, you have to allow God to pour back into you. That was something I personally had to learn. Refueling involves spending time in the Lord's presence. It is the devotion time that you thought was not important. It is the morning and evening prayer that you decided you did not need. It is the Bible study that you chose not to attend or the church service that you slept in on. Refueling is your personal time with God so that He can minister to you. It is your spiritual version of self-care.

We have to take the time to draw closer to God, especially once we have come out of battle, because it is just as easy

CHAPTER 5: REFUELING

for the enemy to sneak his venom into your empty cup if you are not careful. How disheartening would it be to claim a victory, but because you did not take all the steps necessary to seal that victory, you realize that you let all of that hard work slip through your hands. I think about athletes who run in their perspective races. They work so hard to find their rhythm, to pace themselves, to condition their bodies, and as they see the finish line only steps from them, they begin to celebrate their victory only to have the runner behind them take it from them because they were more focused and determined to finish the race. Finishing the race here means refueling. It means growing closer to God. It takes effort to nurture this relationship. Only you can want it. No matter how much I may want it for you, I cannot make you go after it. God is the author and finisher of our faith. He is the ruler, a supreme being overall. If we truly want to win the battles that we face in life, we must not simply fight, but we must continually prepare ourselves. We have said it before, satan comes to steal, kill and destroy. Just because he lost one battle to you, please do not be fooled. He will attack you again and again until he weakens you. Your best defense is constant refueling.

CHAPTER 5: REFUELING

Seek the Lord while He may be found. Call upon Him while He is near. Fill your cup with the things of Christ so that the enemy will not use your moments of emptiness against you.

MY PRAYER FOR YOU

MY PRAYER FOR YOU

I hope this has been an insightful journey and that you have been able to glean strategies that will help you in any battles you face in life. We can agree that this life is a battlefield. However, it is how you handle each obstacle that determines your level of victory. I truly believe in you but more importantly, I believe in the God we serve. Remember that the key to your victory is your surrender to God. Nurture your relationship through studying His Word, praying to Him often and living a life that is pleasing in His sight.

I want to leave this scripture and prayer with you to encourage you through your journey to grow closer to God and in your transformation into a spiritual warrior. I believe your battles have already been fought and the victories won!

> *So we have not stopped praying for you since we first heard about you. We ask God to give you*

complete knowledge of his will and to give you spiritual wisdom and understanding. Then the way you live will always honor and please the Lord, and your lives will produce every kind of good fruit. All the while, you will grow as you learn to know God better and better. We also pray that you will be strengthened with all his glorious power so you will have all the endurance and patience you need. May you be filled with joy, always thanking the Father. He has enabled you to share in the inheritance that belongs to his people, who live in the light. Colossians 1:9-12

I pray that your desire for God exceeds even your expectation. I pray that as you go through the steps outlined in this book, you also develop and maintain a true relationship with Our Father. I pray that any adversity that comes your way is only an opportunity for you to grow deeper in your knowledge of God. I pray the Lord's resurrection power and Holy Ghost boldness be in you and revealed through you. And most of all, I pray that El Olam (The Everlasting God) protects you, sustains you, sanctifies you and fights each victory for you because you are His child, and He knows your name! Now may the peace of God, which passeth all understanding, guard your hearts and your thoughts in Christ Jesus. God Bless!

APPENDIX

APPENDIX

POWERFUL SCRIPTURES FOR SPIRITUAL WARFARE

1. "Submit yourselves to God. Resist the devil, and he will flee from you" (James 4:7).

2. "You are from God, little children, and have overcome them; because greater is He who is in you than he who is in the world" (1 John 4:4).

3. "For though we live in the world, we do not wage war as the world does. The weapons we fight with are not the weapons of the world. On the contrary, they have divine power to demolish strongholds. We demolish arguments and every pretension that sets itself up against the knowledge of God, and we take captive every thought to make it obedient to Christ" (2 Corinthians 10:3-5).

4. "Be self-controlled and alert. Your enemy the devil prowls around like a roaring lion looking for someone to devour. Resist him, standing firm in the faith" (1 Peter 5:8-9).

5. "No weapon that is formed against you will prosper; and every tongue that accuses you in judgment you will condemn. This is the heritage of the servants of the Lord, and their vindication is from Me, declares the Lord" (Isaiah 54:17).

6. "Put on the full armor of God, so that you can take your stand against the devil's schemes. For our struggle is not against flesh and blood, but against the rulers, against the authorities, against the powers of this dark world and against the spiritual forces of evil in the heavenly realms. Therefore, put on the full armor of God, so that when the day of evil comes, you may be able to stand your ground, and after you have done everything, to stand. Stand firm then, with the belt of truth buckled around your waist, with the breastplate of righteousness in place, and with your feet fitted with the readiness that comes from the gospel of peace. In addition to all this, take up the shield

APPENDIX

of faith, with which you can extinguish all the flaming arrows of the evil one. Take the helmet of salvation and the sword of the Spirit, which is the word of God" (Ephesians 6:11-17.)

7. "In all these things, we are more than conquerors through Him who loved us" (Romans 8:37).

8. "But thanks be to God, who gives us the victory through our Lord Jesus Christ" (1 Corinthians 15:57).

9. "Not by might nor by power, but by My Spirit,' says the Lord of hosts" (Zechariah 4:6).

10. "But the Lord is faithful, and he will strengthen you and protect you from the evil one" (2 Thessalonians 3:3).

11. "Behold, I have given you authority to tread on serpents and scorpions, and over all the power of the enemy, and nothing shall hurt you" (Luke 10:19).

12. "The thief comes only to steal and kill and destroy. I came that they may have life and have it abundantly" (John 10:10).

13. "Truly I tell you, whatever you bind on earth will be bound in heaven, and whatever you lose on earth will be loosed in heaven. Again, truly I tell you that if two of you on earth agree about anything they ask for, it will be done for them by my Father in heaven" (Matthews 18:18-19).

14. "The Lord will cause your enemies who rise against you to be defeated before you. They shall come out against you one way and flee before you seven ways" (Deuteronomy. 28:7).

15. "I have told you these things, so that in me you may have peace. In this world you will have trouble. But take heart! I have overcome the world" (John 16:33).

16. "No temptation has overtaken you except what is common to mankind. And God is faithful; he will not let you be tempted beyond what you can bear. But when you

APPENDIX

are tempted, he will also provide a way out so that you can endure it" (1 Corinthians 10:13).

17. "And you will know the truth, and the truth will set you free" (John 8:32).

18. "Do not be overcome with evil but overcome evil with good" (Rom. 12:21).

19. "And they have conquered him by the blood of the Lamb and by the word of their testimony, for they loved not their lives even unto death" (Revelations12:11).

20. "Fight the good fight of the faith. Take hold of the eternal life to which you were called when you made your good confession in the presence of many witnesses" (1 Timothy 6:12).

21. "... On this rock I will build my church, and the gates of hell shall not prevail against it" (Matthew 16:18).

22. "...the reason the Son of God appeared was to destroy the devil's work" (1 John 3:8).

APPENDIX

23. "But they who wait for the Lord shall renew their strength; they shall mount up with wings like eagles; they shall run and not be weary; they shall walk and not faint" (Isiah 40:31).

24. "One of your men puts to flight a thousand, for the Lord your God is He who fights for you, just as He promised you" (Joshua 23:10).

25. "Do not fear them, for the Lord your God is the one fighting for you" (Deuteronomy 3:22).

26. "What then shall we say to these things? If God is for us, who is against us" (Rom. 8:31)?

27. "Through You we will push back our adversaries, through Your name we will trample down those who rise up against us" (Ps. 44:5).

28. "Have I not commanded you? Be strong and courageous! Do not tremble or be dismayed, for the Lord your God is with you wherever you go" (Josh. 1:9).

APPENDIX

29. "For You have girded me with strength for battle; You have subdued under me those who rose up against me" (Ps. 18:39).

30. "He who dwells in the shelter of the Most High will rest in the shadow of the Almighty. I will say of the Lord, He is my refuge and my fortress, my God, in whom I trust. Surely, he will save you from the fowler's snare and from the deadly pestilence. He will cover you with his feathers, and under his wings you will find refuge; his faithfulness will be your shield and rampart..." (Ps. 91:1-4).

31. "This is what the Lord says to you: 'Do not be afraid or discouraged because of this vast army. For the battle is not yours, but God's" 2 (Chron. 20:15).

WORDS OF WAR

WORDS OF WAR

Dunamis – *strength, power, ability*

Exousia – *delegated influence, authority, jurisdiction, liberty, power, right, strength*

Kratos – *force, strength, power, might: mighty with great power; dominion*

Koah – *strength, power, might*

Energia – *energy*

Ischus – *ability, force, strength, might*

Rhema – *that which is or has been uttered by the living voice, thing spoken, word*

Shabach – *to address in a loud tone, i.e. (specifically) loud; figuratively, to pacify (as if by words):--commend, glory, keep in, praise, still, triumph*

Omnipotence – *All-powerful God*

Omniscience – *All-knowing God*

Omnipresence – *Present God Who is everywhere at the same time*

APPENDIX

Kairos - *opportune or seasonable time*

Metron – *measure of rule*

Providential – *divine provision*

Decree - *an official order issued by a legal authority*

Declare - *to make known; set forth*

Legislate - *to make or enact a law or laws*

Government - *administration of life in an organized society as well as the body of officials that presides over the process*

Principalities and Powers - *two names or titles given to spiritual forces, along with authorities, and rulers*

Rulers of Darkness - *these beings are a part of the rank of the kingdom of darkness and include fallen angels that were kicked out of heaven with satan*

Strong, James. Strong's Exhaustive Concordance of the Bible. Abingdon Press, 1890. Print.

NAMES OF GOD

NAMES OF GOD

Elohim – *God the Creator (Genesis 1:1)*

Yahweh (Jehovah) – *I Am, The Self-Existent One, The Lord (Exodus 3:14-15)*

El Elyon - *God Most High (Psalm 7:17)*

El Roi – *The God Who Sees Me (Genesis 16:13-14)*

Adonai – *Lord and Master (Psalm 16:2)*

El Shaddai – *The All-Sufficient One, God Almighty (Genesis 17:1-2)*

El Olam - *The Everlasting God or The Eternal God (Genesis 21:32-33)*

Yahweh-Yier (Jehovah Jireh) – *The Lord Will Provide (Genesis 22:13-14)*

Yahweh (Jehovah) Rapha - *The Lord Who Heals Us Exodus 15:26)*

Yahweh (Jehovah) Nissi - *The Lord Is My Banner (Exodus 17:15)*

APPENDIX

El Qanna (Kannah) – *Consuming Fire, Jealous God (Exodus 34-14)*

Jehovah M'kaddesh (Mekadesh) - *The Lord Who Sanctifies Us (Exodus 31:12-14)*

Yahweh (Jehovah) Shalom - *The Lord Is Peace (Judges 6:24)*

Qedosh Yisrael – *Holy One of Israel (Leviticus 19:1-2)*

Yahweh (Jehovah) Tsuri – *The Lord is My Rock (Psalm 7:17)*

Yahweh (Jehovah) Roi – *The Lord is My Shepherd (Psalm 23:1-4)*

Yahweh (Jehovah) Shammah – *The Lord is There (Exekiel 48:35)*

Miqweh Yisrael – *Hope of Israel (Psalm 71:5)*

Magen - *The Lord is My Shield (Psalm 3:3)*

Migdol-Oz – *My Strong Tower (Proverbs 18:10)*

Atik Yomin – *The Ancient of Days (Daniel 7:9)*

Basileus Basileon – *The King of Kings (Revelation 19:16)*

APPENDIX

El Sali - *The Lord My Strength (Psalm 8:1)*

Yatsar – *The Potter (Isaiah 64:8)*

Abba, Pater – *Father (2 Corinthians 6:18)*

Yahweh (Jehovah) Hesed – *God of Forgiveness (Nehemiah 9:17)*

Jehovah Sabaoth - *The Lord of Hosts (1 Samuel 1:3)*

Jehovah Raah - *The Lord Is My Shepherd (Psalm 23:1)*

Yahweh Tsidqenu/Jehovah Tsidkenu - *The Lord Our Righteousness (Jeremiah 23:6)*

Ish – *Husband (Hosea 2:16,19-20)*

Immanuel – *God With Us (Matthew 1:22-23)*

Iatros – *Physician (Matthew 11:5)*

Alpha kai Omega – *Alpha and Omega (Revelation 22:13)*

O'Reilly, Karen. "30 Powerful Hebrew Names of God and Their Meaning (Free Printable)." Scriptural Grace, 30 Dec. 2020, scripturalgrace.com/post/30-powerful-hebrew-names-of-god-and-their-meaning-free-printable

I am delighted and grateful that you chose to add "Train Our Hands to War" to your library. As a special thank you, I have added a place for you to write your thoughts, favorite scriptures and to compose your own prayers. I hope this book will serve as a tool that you will use over and over again to overcome the wiles of the enemy.

APPENDIX

Notes

APPENDIX

APPENDIX

APPENDIX

APPENDIX

APPENDIX

FAVORITE SCRIPTURES

Favorite Scriptures

List your favorite scriptures. This is a great way to commit them to memory and to further utilize this guide as a tool of warfare.

_____

_____

_____

_____

_____

_____

_____

_____

_____

_____

_____

_____

_____

_____

APPENDIX

APPENDIX

APPENDIX

APPENDIX

APPENDIX

PRAYERS

Prayers

It is important that you begin formulating your own prayers around the written Word of God. Here is your opportunity to take what you have learned and apply it to your situation:

_____

_____

_____

_____

_____

_____

_____

_____

_____

_____

_____

_____

_____

_____

_____

APPENDIX

APPENDIX

APPENDIX

APPENDIX

APPENDIX

ABOUT THE AUTHOR

ABOUT THE AUTHOR

Minister Debbie L. Reid is a wife, mother, ordained minister, author, and entrepreneur. She is certified in several victim's advocacy programs and works with various charitable organizations within her community. Minister Debbie's love for Christ and passion for people fuels her desire to reach the broken and downtrodden through encouragement, ministry, counseling, and LOVE. Although pain knows no boundaries, she truly believes love conquerors all.

In addition to her latest book, *Train Our Hands to War*, Minister Debbie has written and published an inspirational fiction book entitled, *Shedding Silent Tears*. She is working on other inspirational fiction books and plans to publish them in the near future. Through writing, her dream is to build and restore hope to the hearts of people of all ages, nationalities, and genders.

www.ingramcontent.com/pod-product-compliance
Lightning Source LLC
Chambersburg PA
CBHW070948180426
43194CB00041B/1749